SMILE
FROM THE
INSIDE

A Chakra Meditation
When Feeling Out of Control

Sherry Aragosa

Illustrator Ashley McLaughlin

Smiling
Publishers

Smile From the Inside: A Chakra Meditation When Feeling Out of Control © 2020 Smiling Publishers

ISBN 978-1-7348205-0-8 (paperback)

For information regarding permission, write to:

Smiling Publishers

www.sherryfragosa.com

First paperback edition April 2020

Cover and Book Illustration © 2020 Ashley McLaughlin
Cover and book design by Michelle Radomski at One Voice Can
Editing by Zebra Ink
Author photography by Pamela Parker

To Roman,
and the smiles we create ♥♥

This book is a present for YOU, a very special You!

I know that sometimes you may feel things that don't feel good. You may feel out of control...feeling and thinking so many things all at once...like nervous, hurt, angry, sad, and left out.

Did you know that YOU can change those feelings into JOYFUL ones that make you smile?

It is easy.

The first thing to do is take a DEEP breath.

Try it: Take a slow, deep breath in and fill your chest up! Hold your breath, count 1, 2, 3 and then slowly breathe out. Breathing out is called EXHALE. Great job!

Try that one more time. Take a slow, deep breath in and fill your chest up! Hold your breath for 1, 2, 3 and then slowly breathe out, or exhale.

The second thing to do is what really changes your feelings and thoughts. It is called a chakra meditation.

"What is a Chakra Meditation?" What a great question! Let me explain. First, what is a chakra besides a funny sounding word?

CROWN CHAKRA

HEART CHAKRA

SOLAR PLEXUS CHAKRA

ROOT CHAKRA

Chakras are a part of you that you can feel and do not see. They are made up of feelings and thoughts. They spin in a spiral. The spiral begins inside of us and reaches out far and wide.

What is a Meditation? A meditation is something you imagine, like a dream. You think of things and you see them in your mind.

Now let's try a Chakra Meditation together. We will imagine your chakras feeling and thinking all good things.

To feel happy and full of joy, to feel focused and calm, to *Smile from the Inside,* to feel safe and strong, to feel love and to feel loved, to feel confident.

To get rid of feeling scared, feeling nervous, feeling shy, feeling angry, feeling sad, feeling unhappy.

Simply Breathe and Imagine.

This special meditation will use 4 chakras to change your feelings to happy ones, and let you *Smile from the Inside.*

Step One: Open your Crown Chakra.

In your imagination, see your Crown Chakra on the top of your head.

This friendly swirling spiraling cloud, made of white sparkling light, shoots from your head above you.

Take a large breath in and feel the peaceful joyful energy swirling with strength and with ease.

Exhale and feel your Crown and your breath shoot up towards the sky, the heavens, the Sun, and the Moon.

What would you like to connect your Crown to today?

Clouds? Moon? Sun? People around the world? Stars? The Universe? You choose.

As you take another slow deep breath in, feel your Crown Chakra grow and surround the thing you chose a minute ago. Hold your breath for 1, 2, 3, and exhale.

See the friendly white sparkling spiraling cloud shooting from your head above you.

Can you feel your emotions calm to a peaceful space? Your head feels light and lifts high off your shoulders as you sit taller. Your thoughts are calm, and your body feels full of smiles.

Step Two: Open your Root Chakra.

In your imagination, see your Root Chakra below you.

This friendly swirling spiraling cloud, made of warm red light, shoots from your seat below you, deep down to the middle of the Earth.

Take a large breath in and feel the strong gentle energy swirling with strength and with ease.

Exhale and feel your Root and your breath shoot down towards the Earth below your feet. Imagine your strong gentle Root Chakra flowing like roots of trees down into the Earth.

What would you like to connect your Root to today?

Grass? Sand? Water in the rivers and oceans? Mountains? Tree roots? Rocks deep inside the Earth? You choose.

As you take another slow deep breath in, feel your Root Chakra grow and surround the thing you chose a minute ago. Hold your breath for 1, 2, 3, and exhale.

See the friendly red spiraling cloud shooting from your body below you.

You feel safe, calm and strong. Your head feels light and lifts high off your shoulders as you sit taller. Your body feels strong and rooted in your seat. Your thoughts are calm and you feel full of smiles.

Step Three: Open your Heart Chakra.

In your imagination, see your Heart Chakra inside your chest. This friendly swirling spiraling cloud, made of bright green light, shoots from your heart, in front of you and in back of you.

Take a large breath in and feel the joyful, loving, happy energy swirling with strength and with ease.

Exhale and feel your Heart and your breath shoot out one mile in front of and in back of you. Imagine your joyful happy Heart connecting with the Hearts of all the people and animals around you.

What would you like to connect your Heart to today?

Plants? A person? A group of people? Animals? A symbol of a Heart that grows larger and larger and larger? You choose.

As you take another slow deep breath in, feel your Heart Chakra grow and surround the thing you chose a minute ago. Hold your breath for 1, 2, 3, and exhale.

See the friendly bright green spiraling cloud shooting from your body in front of you and in back of you.

You feel happy, and full of love and joy.

Your head feels light and lifts high off your shoulders as you sit taller. Your strong, rooted body feels joyful, and full of love. Your thoughts are kind and calm and you feel full of smiles.

Step Four: Open your Solar Plexus Chakra.

In your imagination, see your Solar Plexus at the top of your belly.

This friendly swirling spiraling cloud, made of glittery yellow light, shoots from your center, in front of you and in back of you.

Take a large breath in and feel who you are, a kind and strong person. Feel this with strength and with ease.

Exhale and feel your Solar Plexus and your breath shoot out one mile in front of you and in back of you. Imagine sharing your kindness and strength with all that surrounds you.

What would you like to connect your Solar Plexus to today?

Remember that you are made up of LOVE and JOY. Can you imagine connecting to love and joy? A good way to do that is saying a Mantra which is a statement you repeat to yourself.

A good one for you would be to repeat:

"I am love, I am love, I am love." "I am joy, I am joy, I am joy."

As you take another slow deep breath in, feel your Solar Plexus Chakra grow and hear it say, "I am Love." Hold your breath for 1, 2, 3, and exhale.

See the friendly glittery yellow spiraling cloud shooting from your body in front of you and in back of you.

I AM LOVE

You feel strong, kind, calm and full of joy. Your head feels light and lifts high off your shoulders as you sit taller. Your strong, rooted body feels joyful, and full of love. Your thoughts are kind and calm and you feel full of smiles.

Your chakras are open and connected!

You are balanced, strong, kind, full of love and connected to YOU.

Smile on the inside and the outside.
Share your love, joy and smiles.

About the Author...

Always being sensitive to the environment around her, plus having a love for nature and all things natural, Sherry began her exploration into energy medicine and chakras as a young girl in rural Eastern Pennsylvania. As life began to challenge her, she dove deeper into chakras and energy to find her joy.

At 21 years old, moving to the Phoenix metropolis in Arizona allowed for her to add formal training in chakra balancing, reiki, massage therapy and holistic health to her business training and BA in Behavioral Science. Utilizing chakra balancing in her everyday home life and business life, added real world applications of immeasurable value.

Being a licensed massage therapist for over 20 years and co-creating and running a natural OB/GYN office for over 15 years, she has observed, practiced and learned many intricacies of the way our chakras and energy mold and dictate our everyday actions. Sherry feels and lives her Truth: that having the ability to open the energy in the chakra system at challenging times and times of focused manifestation, allows for truly amazing transformations to develop in a very simple to-do package. She feels that anyone, young or old; religious, spiritual or skeptical; happy, sad or indifferent; can and will feel a change within them by influencing their chakra system. Her goal is to share the knowledge she has gathered with children and adults, so that everyone has an easier path to joy, and to *Smile from the Inside.*

Resources:

Visit www.sherryfragosa.com for the following:

• Parent Guides to assist in getting the most out of this book

• Chakra and Emotions activities for kids

• And more!